JOANNE OPPENHEIM

RON BRODA

HAVE YOU SEEN

BUGS?

Scholastic Canada Ltd.

Scholastic Canada Ltd.
175 Hillmount Road, Markham, Ontario L6C 1Z7
Scholastic Inc.
555 Broadway, New York, NY 10012, USA
Scholastic Australia Pty Limited
PO Box 579, Gosford, NSW 2250, Australia
Scholastic New Zealand Limited
Private Bag 94407, Greenmount, Auckland, New Zealand
Scholastic Ltd.
Villiers House, Clarendon Avenue, Leamington Spa,
Warwickshire CV32 5PR, UK

To Toni.
—J.O.
To my own little bugs, Taylor and Eden Broda.
—R.B.

The illustrator would like to thank Joanne Webb for her help with page 30 — what a great idea! Thanks also to William Kuryluk for a wonderful job on the photography.

The illustrations for this book were made with paper sculpture and watercolour. Each layer of paper was cut, formed and painted before being glued into place. The finished sculptures were then carefully lit and photographed to create the final image.

Photography by William Kuryluk.

Canadian Cataloguing in Publication Data
Oppenheim, Joanne
Have you seen bugs?
ISBN 0-590-12496-X
1. Insects — Juvenile literature. I. Broda, Ron. II. Title.
Q1467.2.066 1998 j595.7 C98-930730-1

First paperback edition, 1998.

5 4 3 2 Printed and bound in Canada 8 9/9 0 1 2 3 4 /0

Have you seen bugs?

Itty-bitty bugs
small as specks of sand,

wide-winged bugs
bigger than your hand.

Bugs with stripes
or speckles
or spots,
shiny like metal
or covered with dots.

Iridescent bugs
that shimmer in the light,

winking, blinking bugs
that twinkle in the night.

Dark as bark
green as grass
see-through bugs
with wings like glass.

Shaped like thorns
or sticks
or leaves,

burrowed in bubbles
or clinging to trees.

Hide-and-seek bugs —
can you see these?

Watch out! for these show-off bugs
with colours bold and bright.
Flashy, sassy, daring bugs
such easy bugs to sight!

Like warning signs,
bold markings say:
I'm poison! I smell!
I sting! Stay away!

Have you seen bugs
and how they move?

Long-legged bugs
jumping with a bound,
short-legged bugs
running on the ground.

Some are fast:
they dart and leap;
some are slow:
they crawl and creep.

Bugs that flutter
and scurry
and dive,
bugs that buzz around a hive.

Walking on the ceiling,
crawling up a wall —
some bugs hardly move at all!

What about water bugs?
Walking-on-the-water bugs
swimming-under-water bugs
skimming-over-water bugs.

Oaring, soaring,
whirling, twirling,
striding, gliding.
Have you seen these?

Have you heard bugs?

Bugs have no voices
but still they can sing,
rubbing their legs,
whirring their wings.

Busy crickets in thickets
wait for night to fall,
then they rub their legs together
and chirp their mating call.

A bug has no ears
on its little bug head,
but some bugs hear
through their legs instead!
While others use antennae

to taste and hear and smell,
and tiny hairs that touch and tell
and help them find their mates as well.
Some bugs even use their feet
to take a taste before they eat!

Have you seen bugs
and how they eat?

Beetles have mouths —
they can bite and chew and snip,
while others like the butterfly
have mouths with straws that sip.

Most bugs dine on plants,
some bugs dine on meat,
others take a nip of blood
or sip on nectar sweet.

Have you seen baby bugs?

Inside a hive,
nesting in hair,

bugs hatch from eggs
everywhere.

Underwater, underground,
in so many places
bug eggs are found.

In the bark of trees
or wrapped up in leaves,
baby bugs hatch
from all of these!

Baby bugs are small,
but just for a bit.
Little bugs keep growing
till their skins don't fit.

But some bugs form a chrysalis
or spin a fine cocoon,
where abracadabra! they grow wide wings
in a magical changing room.

Have you seen working bugs?
From flower to flower,
bugs work as they go,

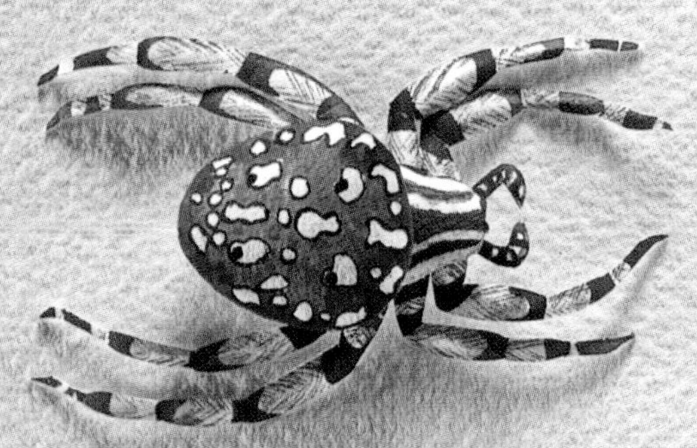

carrying pollen
that makes gardens grow.
If it weren't for bugs,
orchards would be bare!
You couldn't have an apple,
an orange or a pear.
There wouldn't be corn
or pumpkins or wheat;
without bugs we'd have little to eat.

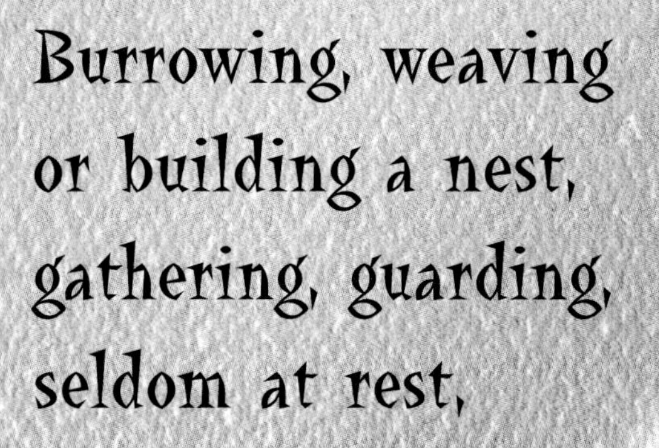

Burrowing, weaving
or building a nest,
gathering, guarding,
seldom at rest,

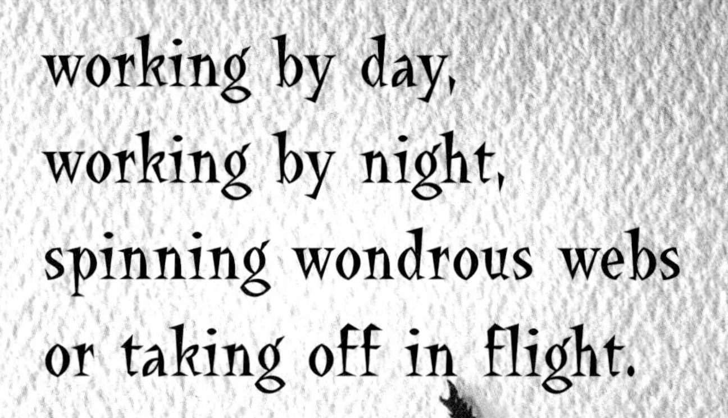

working by day,
working by night,
spinning wondrous webs
or taking off in flight.

Sleek as a needle,
furry as a bear,
so many kinds of bugs
living everywhere!
An army of ants
a flurry of fleas
a band of moths
a swarm of bees
billions of bugs . . .
Have you seen these?

USA

The big tree is very old now, but still strong and growing. With a bit of luck, and clean air and water, it will go on shading picnics for many more years.